Dedicated to the plastic heart, analog soul, grand history and bright future of the Diana, Diana+ and Diana F+ cameras.

Prologue

Dear Lomographer, photo-hunter, camera collector, and analog-lover,

We do not know which act of providence brought you here. But we can safely assume that you do not know what you're in for. Taking a trip through the illustrious realms of the Diana, Diana+, and DianaF+ is by no means an organized journey. You'll find yourself alone and a bit confused – facing the most wild, exciting, dangerous, charming, sinful, and unforeseeable adventures and opportunities ahead of you. We're here to give you a few instructions and tips for your travels, to keep you company under a shady olive tree, and to show you the way if you find yourself stranded and clueless between Heaven and Hell, good and bad, appearance and reality, happiness and sorrow, or endless Diana-analog merrymakings and the eternal, virtual nothing!

In short, this book includes everything that you need to stay on the right path:

- The wonderful story of the original Diana – given to use in the late 60's as a simple, pure, and all-plastic photographic tool – and its

2007 rebirth as the shining Diana+ camera, complete with pinhole power and other all-new capabilities.

- The crucial insights, and dazzling images of Mark Sink, Allan Detrich, Tony Lim, and Cat Ong – four dyed-in-the-wool Diana experts.

- Building on the ten Vignettes presented in our first Diana+ book, we're thrilled to present an all-new selection, as written by Michael Kuhle, Sarah Zucker, Nick Counts, and Regina Belmonte.

- A soaring overview of the Diana's many different and ravishing faces - in the form of Allan Detrich's stunning Diana & Diana clone collection. [Pay close attention here, as the Diana is apt to change her colors many times again in the future.]

- Quite a bit of useful information about Lomography and the Western and Eastern Societies of Lomographers – which hereby gratefully submit to the Diana's powerful regency.

- And most importantly of all: a breathtaking preview of the Diana+ and DianaF+'s unrestrained artistic capabilities. Throughout this book is a flood of gorgeous photos taken through the lens of the Diana+ cameras and composed by a brave and diligent contingent of Lomographic Society members. As you take in the splendour of these images, you can imagine how deeply our love runs for this camera – and you can expect to see countless more of them in future books and online galleries.

So there you are. And here we stand – with arms open and hearts in eager anticipation of YOUR divine encounters with the heavenly Diana, Diana+, and DianaF+. Following your review and digestion of the content within this book, it behooves you to take matters into your own hands and document your own Diana visions through YOUR PICTURES and YOUR DIANA VIGNETTES – which can be readily shared with your fellow Lomographers at
www.lomography.com/diana

We await you,
Your Society of Lomographers

Introduction

The Big Picture (Forget All About It)

Seriously, just put it all out of your mind. We'll no longer "look for the big picture," and there will be no more "getting an overview" or "stepping back to take it all in." All of these concepts imply an abrupt halt to activity - a conscious pause of your natural drive and instincts. As we say day in and day out: Be fast. Who's got the time to consider the implications when close to a million tremendous potential photos are streaming right past your nose? No Diana owner worth their chops would spend one iota of energy on the big picture when there are so many crucial elements to focus on.

To hold, point, and shoot a Diana camera implies a conscious decision to relinquish control. To concentrate your creative powers on capturing the moment and telling a story - rather than fiddling with a bunch of knobs and levers. A blurry-soft and dreamy-toned Diana image is more an interpretation of reality than a correct representation of it. In a way, it's somehow more accurate to compare the Diana to an oily vintage typewriter than to a megapixel machine of today. With each click of the shutter, a moment is captured in a unique and fairly unpredictable way - and a small narrative begins to reveal itself. As the viewer, you're invited to read into it and interpret it in your own way. On top of that, you can count yourself as an individual note in the Diana's illustrious history - which dates back to the better part of 40 years.

The Grand History of the Diana Camera

Back in the 1960's, a small firm in Hong Kong – the Great Wall Plastics Factory – created a dirt-cheap 120 camera called the "Diana." Crafted entirely of plastic, each camera cost about a dollar. As a mainstream product, the Diana was pretty much a failure – and was discontinued in the 1970's. But like any superstar cut down in their prime, the Diana's posthumous appeal skyrocketed. As a cult artistic tool of avant-garde and lo-fi photographers, it was a rousing success! They loved its soft & dreamy images, super-saturated colors, unpredictable blurring, and random contrast. Diana shots are raw & gritty, with a character all their own. They simply cannot be duplicated by any other camera on Earth! In short order, the Diana rose to prominence as one of the most treasured and sought-after cult analog cameras from the late 70's onward.

The Diana+ & Diana F+ Camera

Ever look at a majestic classic car and wish that you could walk down to the dealership and pickup such a beauty brand new? That's pretty much sums up our feelings when we came across the Diana.

Who could resist the charms of its plastic body? How could you not absolutely love its lo-fi masterpiece photos? Something this beautiful, this classic, and this crucial to the world of analog photography shouldn't have suffered such an early demise. And since we had the means, the knowledge, and the opportunity to rebuild the Diana from the ground up (with a few extras tossed in) - the Lomography Diana+ was born in 2007. The Diana's original charms (radiant color-dripping lens, soft-focus surprises, all-plastic body, dead-simple shutter) were expertly duplicated to provide the authentic look n' feel of the original. On top of that, brand new Pinhole & Endless Panorama features were added into the mix – thereby paving the way for an entirely new class of Diana images and techniques! Hot on the heels of Lomography's initial Diana+ was the DianaF+, an awesome recreation of the rare Diana flash model. From the silver-surfer tones of the flash, to its old-school "dual pins" metal connection plug, the DianaF+ is absolutely dripping with authentic sixties style. Not to mention, that flash kicks out a pretty fierce light!

This book is a testament the to grand history of the original Diana and to the bright & limitless future of the Diana+, DianaF+, and many more models to come!

Dive into the Details

The Diana loves the little things. It loves breakfast, your dog, your boyfriend or girlfriend, that crazy hat in the window, the unbeliev-able morning traffic, those gummed-up salt shakers, a blazing afternoon sun, your nose when it's all close-up and blurry, the shoes that you didn't buy, and your hamburger-champion uncle. Its lightweight plastic body feels good next to yours, and it doesn't bog you down with a lot of weight. Diana's true soul is that of a lithe, athletic huntress. With a stealthy gait, she quietly stalks her prey and waits for the precise moment to strike. She's happy with big game or small game, so it doesn't matter if you shoot a dramtic life-changing event or a nonsensical, pants-free dance around the room. Keep the lens on for the classic look or strip it off for a soft-focus pinhole portrait. No matter what, she always yields evocative photos.

Looking for the big picture means missing the individual parts, and that just won't do at all. The real spice of life is waiting right there for you to capture it, and it's passing you by every second; with the Diana, you'll not only capture and document these fleeting moments, but you'll do so with a style that cannot be imitated, and a unique ability to reach into your subject and tell a gripping story. We call these little tales - all of which can be told with a click of Diana's shutter - a vignette.

Your Mission & Our Plans

As you read through the rest of this book, keep in mind that Diana's powers, charms, heart, and soul are all in your hands. After all, you've got a charming plastic camera sitting in front of you, right? This is a radically unique tool, one that will allow you to capture some of the greatest images that you've ever witnessed. Don't place it up on a mantle to collect dust, or put it in the back of a drawer, or lock it in the glove compartment, or any of that nonsense. Keep it with you at all times, and hold it close - you never know when a crucial Diana moment will arrive. And when it does, you've got a job to do.

More Diana Books to Come

Feel this page between your fingers. My god, is there anything sweeter than that? There are few pleasures on Earth that compare with slipping your eyeballs over a radiant photo book, especially one so densely packed with mind-blowing images and content. This book is just the beginning. We hereby pledge to roll forward with a steady stream of new Diana books in the future – which will be all about you. We're going to show your photos, tell your stories, share your most intimate Diana knowledge, and compile a series of fat, CMYK-printed testaments to the explosive development and unleashed intensity of the Diana and Diana+ communities.

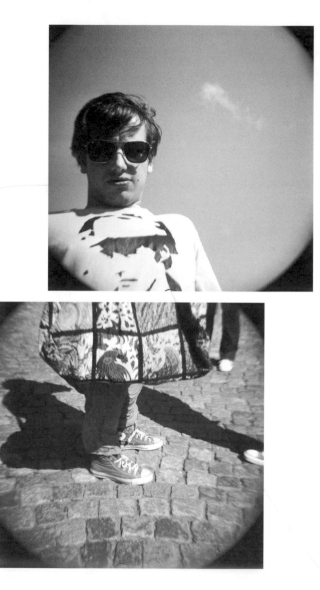

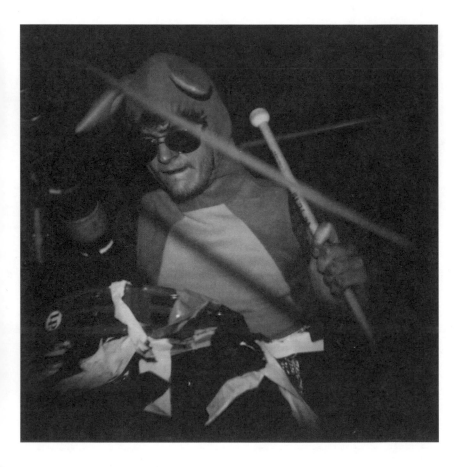

Diana Vignettes & the Diana World Tour

The Diana Vignettes

Rigidly defined, a vignette is a "short, impressionistic scene that focuses on one moment or gives a particular insight into a character, idea, or setting." A vignette is brief, but complex; bite-size, but extremely satisfying. With merely a few words and a few specific details, it gives you a penetrating view into the life and motivations of your subject. In photographic circles, vignetting refers to the progressive darkening of an image at the edges of the frame - an effect for which the Diana is world-famous.

Unlike any other camera on Earth, the Diana is prized for its power to tell a narrative through its unique and otherworldly images. Every dreamlike shot is bursting at the seams with character and content. If a typical image tells a thousand words, then a Diana shot tells somewhere in the realm of 6 or 7 million (give or take a few).

The tales that will follow celebrate this fact. Just as the Diana captures a tell-all vignette of your subject with every click of its shutter, we've captured a collection of sample Diana Vignettes and accompanying images to define the true soul of our beloved Diana. You'll find them sprinkled throughout the rest of this book in several bite-sized portions. These tales are intended to whet your appetite, for we'll soon be expecting your full participation in the most ambitious contest in the history of plastic cameras...

The Diana Vignettes Photo & Writing Challenge!

Friends and Lomographers, we have entered a brand-new era! Lomography has gone into the world of literature, combining pictures and short stories: the Diana Vignettes. We're now thrilled to give you the opportunity to fully explore the fascinating capabilities of your Diana+, DianaF+, your sharp eyesight, keen instincts, and creative writing skills. There are two ways to participate:

1) Submit your images

A steady stream of Diana Vignettes will give you an elaborate and literary "assignment" - which you'll interpret and illustrate with your Diana+ or DianaF+ images. You'll have to juice your creativity for every drop that you can squeeze out. After all, it's not easy to depict a hot love affair on a Greek Island if it's January in Milwaukee. Use a classic Diana-style image, or toss it up with a newfangled pinhole or endless panorama shot. But with a little ingenuity, and a lot of faith in the all-plastic-power of your Diana, it's entirely possible!

2) Submit your own Diana Vignette stories

Got a bit of a writing bug? Feel like creating short story about the Diana+? We are looking for your craziest and most unexpected short stories. All stories need to be written in English. Don't worry, you don't necessarily need to be an A-Student in English — it's more important that the overall concept and characters are extremely interesting. Look over your collection of Diana snapshots — do you see a story brewing in there? If your story is chosen as a Diana Vignette, you can then submit the very images that inspired its creation!

Great prizes and worldwide Lomographic fame await you! Even before you press down that Diana shutter release for the first time, head over to our Diana Vignettes site and see what's in store: **http://www.lomography.com/diana/diana-vignettes**

The Diana Vignettes World Tour

Don't think for a second that all the incredible Diana Vignette images from around the world are merely going to sit on their laurels and take up bandwidth on the Lomography.com servers. They'll quickly be put to task in an upcoming and ongoing tour of Lomographic hotspots around the globe. Jumping from one city to the next, the World Tour will be a traveling exhibition that showcases the very finest of Diana Vignette images & stories alongside a primo selection of our classic "Detrich Collection" original Diana & Diana clone cameras. Stay tuned at the Diana+ microsite (**www.lomography.com/diana**) for more details.

Diana Vignettes I

Amanda Watts Goes Into the [London] Wild
By Michael Kuhle (username: michaelkuhle)

Tent. Compass. Sleeping bag. Rice. Matches. Steel pot. Beef jerky. Sharp knife. Lip balm. Amanda took her time and meticulously checked each item off of her list. If you want to break the bonds of society and enjoy the bold taste of sweet freedom that only Mother Nature can provide, then you've got to be prepared. Amanda had quite enough of the relentless hustle of London. She had one too many hectic days at work. Five too many sweaty and slow rides on the tube. And about three hundred too many ready-made sandwiches at Tesco express. She was going to leave it all behind. She was going into the wild.

If you looked back a few months earlier, you'd find a much different person than the radicalized naturist that she became. Once upon a time, Amanda held down a pretty solid job at a prestigious London public relations firm. She handled fashion accounts, which mostly involved the constant distribution of free gifts and subtle bribes to stylish magazine fashion editors. This job – glamorous enough for a lead character on "Sex and the City" - would be a dream position for many girls. At first she liked it – especially the parties, dinners, and little weekend junkets that always came on the company's dime. But little by little, things began to wear on her. She quickly grew tired of her fast-paced life, and yearned to get in touch with the elements. With the Earth! As a private-school student and card-carrying member of the upwardly mobile, she had precious little experience with living the simple life. The only way out was to make a clear break with society. On Monday, she was at work until her usual end time of 6:30. On Tuesday, she was nowhere to be seen. Her phone was cancelled, her apartment was vacant, and she had hit the road.

Amanda surveyed her options carefully. Although she longed for the wild, heading to the jungle, rainforest or [gasp] northern reaches of Alaska was a bit out of her depth. Everyone has to start somewhere, and she kept her valid tube pass for the month. She boarded the District line with all of her gear, and shot off towards Richmond Park. At a size of nearly 2500 acres, the park was large enough for her to lose the crowds, and was also home to primo game: over 650 free roaming deer. If she nailed a few of them for her own food and survival, who was going to notice if that number went down to 647 or so?

This was one of the most exciting adventures of her entire life! As such, Amanda wanted to document all of her trials and tribulations. In keeping with the "back-to-basics" approach, she packed a Diana+ camera along – a freebee that she received in a PR-event giftbag a few months back. She'd grown to like its off-kilter photos, and the Diana's sheer simplicity matched her overall rejection of modern society and technology.

Conscious to avoid the crowds, Amanda searched out a spot within the park. She walked past the playgrounds, horse trails, outdoor restaurants, bicycle paths, and every other mark of civilization, and pitched her tent in a semi-secluded circle of trees. This was to be her outpost, where she would live the next two years of her life, depending on only her wits and cunning to survive. Her first day was absolute bliss! She foraged for kindling, started a fire, and celebrated with a hearty meal of rice. Of course, she documented everything around her, and took a few stretched-arm self-portraits of her mile-wide grin.

Over the course of the week, however, the appeal of this "wild life" began to wane. Although bathing in Pen Pond was refreshing, the water stank a bit after she got out. Rice tasted great to her for the first day, good for the second, and kind of terrible by the third.

It also turned out that hunting deer with a pocket knife was exceptionally difficult. Not once did a deer stand still long enough to be stabbed by any of Amanda's wild flailing. They weren't nearly as dumb as they look. As her rice ration wore thin, her food options were narrowing to mystery berries on the tress or just straight-up eating grass. The wafting smell of bacon rolls at nearby Pembroke Lodge wasn't helping either.

Throughout her seven days of hunting, gathering, gazing at the trees, marveling at the skies, viewing tourists from afar, and sleeping under the stars, Amanda kept a running visual diary with her Diana+ and a sack of 120 film. As hunger pangs set in and she felt herself weakening (and in psychotic want for a chicken pot pie), she photographed her own looks of yearning and semi-starvation. Although her will wanted to stay, her body was giving in. Until one morning, after a full week of "wild" living, Amanda was gone. To where, no one really knew.

The Park Police weren't too surprised when they happened upon Amanda's encampment. This was far from the first time that a vagrant or hippie squatter tried to forge a home inside their idyllic reserve. As they rooted through the things she left behind, they were surprised to find a chunky plastic camera and what looked to be 20-odd rolls of exposed medium format film. "No problem" said one of the officers, "we've got a development lab down at the main stationhouse. We'll run these through, and see who our illegal visitor was."

Lizzie the Antique Shop Spelunker
By Sarah Zucker (username: thesarahshow)

"Ouch."

Lizzie Feldspar instinctively put her finger in her mouth. Her absent-minded habit of running her fingertips along things as she walked had, once again, caused her pain. This time, the source was a jar of glass swizzle sticks, with one precariously placed barbecue skewer among them. It was almost as though someone knew the tactile allure of the colorful knickknacks, and had placed the skewer there to deter those who had trouble keeping their hands to themselves. Lizzie Feldspar was just such a person.

Flick

The soft sound of her Diana camera's shutter flipping over in its dainty plastic body. "There, I caught you." A smile of satisfaction. These trifling trinkets couldn't bully her without a fight. Seeing nothing else of interest on the table, Lizzie moved on.

Lizzie has never known, consciously anyway, why it is that she is so drawn to Antique shops. Just as one never asks why ice cream tastes good, or why puppies are cute, Lizzie hadn't thought to question this affinity of hers. The truth is, like all of us, Lizzie is a lonely girl. Her life has no permanence, and she's nothing more than an insignificant speck on an insignificant speck in a big insignificant Universe. Being among all the debris and remnants of lives past makes her feel like she's part of something bigger; not just one girl, but every girl ever. But Lizzie doesn't know this. She thinks she stops at these places because her mother used to go to them when she was little, and the comfort she pulls from them is nothing more than fond filial remembrance. Very few people concern themselves with matters of Universality in their day-to-day living, and Lizzie is not one of the few.

Flick

Another capture, this time a crystal bowl filled with fake fruits, flaking and crusty with the dust of the ages. Lizzie looks at her Diana, and notices some dust on the lens. She huffs some hot air onto it, and polishes it with her sweater. A photographer by trade would have wept at this sight, but Lizzie's relationship with her camera was far from professional: This was intimacy of the closest kind.

Nearing her 25th birthday, it was now almost ten years since Lizzie and Diana had become a team. The shop where she'd discovered it was not too unlike the one she found herself in presently. Objects and heirlooms heaped and piled on top of old furniture without rhyme or reason being lorded over by a grim shopkeeper, whose eyes lolled in his head surveying his treasures. It was in Virginia, no maybe North Carolina, one of the two. A much-needed stop on an epic road trip from Ohio to Florida. At the time, Lizzie and her siblings still balked at being dragged to a place full of old junk for the sake of seeming like ordinary kids. But they secretly enjoyed the idea of rummaging through other people's discarded items looking for treasure.

Treasure, glorious treasure. They never knew what form it would come to them in, but they knew they wanted it. And, at this one particular shop in Virginia, or North Carolina, or wherever it actually was, Lizzie Feldspar found her treasure. She was walking through the shop, trying to look cool (not realizing that one can never look cool walking through an antique shop), when she saw a crate full of old MAD Magazines on the floor. She bent down to leaf through them, and as she did, found herself staring directly at what appeared to be an empty shelf. It was strange, she thought, that there would be nothing on this shelf in a store where you couldn't see a single clean surface otherwise. So, without thinking, Lizzie reached to the back of the shelf, and felt around. There it was, there in the shadows. A Diana camera, looking shiny and new as the day it had been injection molded and packaged. Lizzie didn't know anything about it at the time, but the minute she saw it, she knew she had to have it.

Flick

An old oil lamp, burning away on a bureau. "This is a good shop," Lizzie thought to herself, "I ought to come back again." She hadn't completed the thought before she heard a grumbling noise coming from the front of the store. She looked up to see the shopkeeper looking down his nose at her, over the top of his glasses the way her piano teacher used to do when she played a heinously wrong note. The man shook his head a little, and Lizzie blushed and put the Diana away. He clearly didn't want her taking pictures in here, perhaps worried that she might steal the soul of his treasure and never return it. Deciding there was nothing there she was bursting to buy, Lizzie made her way silently out of the store.

Her keys seemed nowhere to be found in her pocket, and she was in no hurry, so Lizzie leaned back against her black Honda civic, and took a breath of the crisp Autumn air. She pulled the Diana back out of her purse, and turned it over a couple times in her hands. The black tape she had put on it to keep the light out (a trick she had to learn the hard way) was starting to peel, and she picked at it a little with her fingernails. "Some good finds today," she thought, smiling at the Diana as if she were expecting a response. Many people have a fault of treating people like objects, but Lizzie posses the fault of treating objects like people. This is just the way she relates to the world. And so, with one last thankful look at the Diana, she placed it gingerly back in her bag, and politely asked her car for entry. It obliged, and Lizzie Feldspar drove off through the crackling leaves, and on to her next adventure.

History of the Diana

The Myth of the Great Wall Plastic Factory

Like a true legend, the original Diana camera's birth is shrouded in mystery and conjecture. The popular account reads as follows: Back in the early 1960s, a Kowloon Bay, Hong Kong, company called the Great Wall Plastics Factory created an extremely inexpensive and completely plastic compact camera. Called the "Diana," this little beauty was constructed of a lightweight plastic body and a cheap plastic single-element lens. Only the shutter and a few necessary parts were crafted in metal. The original specs consisted of two shutter speeds, three aperture settings, and manual focusing from about 1m to infinity. The original Diana film format was 120, which was quite popular in Asia at the time. It shot 16 4x4cm images per roll.

Diana Clones and Copies

It's assumed that this original Diana met with significant success in its domestic and export markets, so much so that a flood of knockoffs, copies, and derivatives were quickly introduced to capitalize on the demand. With names like "Future Scientist," "Megomatic," "Snappy," "Windsor," and "Zodiac," the clones offered a huge range of varying features, including simplified apertures, extra shutter speeds, electronic flashes, fake light meters, longer lenses, and a 620 film format. Several versions were private-label commissions by large American companies such as GE, Reader's Digest, JC Penny, and Avis Rent-a-Car. It's not clear which copies were made by the original Great Wall Plastic Factory, and which were made by rival manufacturers.

Death of the Dream

As the story goes, production of the Diana and its various clones came to a close in the mid-1970s. As 35mm film and Instamatic cameras grew in popularity, the clumsy roll-film Dianas fell to the wayside. The camera would continue to be widely available for a few more years - often as a free novelty gift or a thrift-store regular - but its days were very much numbered. The march of progress had slain the humble Diana in its wake.

The Loving Afterglow

Just as the Diana was in its final death throes in Asia, it was gaining a new lease on life in the West. Photographers and artists began to realize the full creative potential of these cheapo cameras with their inherent light leaks, lens aberrations, and plastic construction. These visionaries saw the Diana's characteristics not as faults, but as unique abilities to be treasured and vigorously employed. In the Diana, they found a tool to make the boring look intoxicating – and a way to completely let go of control. For many of them – especially established photographers, the unpredictability, cheapness, and insanity of the Diana held an irresistible appeal. Its blurry, leaky, vignetted, and often random images were the cornerstone of many an exhibit and portfolio. As the Diana became more rare and increasingly sought-after, its price skyrocketed from $1.00 at the local thrift shop to $150 on Ebay. Seriously, the guys over at Great Wall would have been kicking themselves in the rear if they knew.

Back from the Ashes (The Diana+ by Lomography)

Ask any Lomographer and they'll quickly tell you about our love for plastic medium format cameras. It began with the Holga, a similarly constructed, yet more modern take on the Diana. Designed in the '80s as a dirt cheap 120 camera, the Holga rose to cult status and attained a huge popularity throughout our international Lomographic community – so much so that we created several extremely successful products and books around it. As interest exploded around the Holga, we began to look into the camera that is misidentified as its predecessor: The Diana.

Ah, we can clearly remember the day when this ironic blue-and-black beauty first arrived at the Lomographic headquarters in Vienna. We had seen photos of it online, but no one in our company had touched one in the flesh. From the second that we held it in our quivering fingers, we fell hopelessly in love. Our first batch of leaky, blurry, dreamy, and definitely slightly screwed up images only served to confirm that warm feeling. It was a kind of magic!

A challenge was set out on our table: How can we supply this incredible item to our loyal Lomographic Community? The initial production had ceased decades ago, so going to the original factory was out of the question. Luckily, our extensive experience with plastic camera design and production equipped us to pull apart the camera and literally rebuild it from the ground up. Like a radiant phoenix, the Diana could rise from the ashes and burn once again in the hearts of true analog-lovers around the world. And they wouldn't have to fork out a ton of money on Ebay to get one.

From the beginning, we decided that our reproduction would have to add something to the original. We weren't out to merely copy the design; rather, we wanted to retain its greatest features and improve upon them. This meant adding all-new functionality to the camera and dramatically expanding its creative potential. We'd call it Diana PLUS.

A factory in China with the tools and expertise was located and contracted for Diana production. The body was re-cast using a duplication of the original mold. The color scheme was tweaked to get that crazy shade of blue just right. The lens was designed and tweaked about a thousand times to obtain that "perfectly imperfect" mix of sharp, blurry, and "What the hell is that?" looks. The variable aperture and variable shutter speeds of the original were built inside. And then we sprinkled some of our very own pixie dust on the whole project to create the following "PLUS" features:

Pinhole Setting
Remove the lens, set the aperture to a super-small pinhole and shoot

a soft-focus, severely old-school image. With a nearly unlimited depth of field, these dreamlike long-exposure photos have a signature look all their own.

Endless Panorama

This is a time-tested Holga favorite, but it's always a bit hard to judge how far to advance. When you use this special setting for the Diana, it places sequential frames right next to each other (well, very close at least - nothing is too precise with the Diana). You can shoot a long, concurrent, and unlimited panoramic image, simply by twisting your body and firing every now and then.

A Shining Star (DianaF+ by Lomography)

As we browsed through the images of classic Diana cameras, it was impossible to resist the charms of the rare Diana flash variants. The oversized electronic flash was nearly half the size of the camera itself – and it came dipped in reflective silver paint to [supposedly] amplify its power. To see the two pieces together was absolutely stunning – a true 1960s throwback. To wield this camera is to look like an all-plastic lo-fi version of Jimmy Olsen, shooting soft-focus and off-kilter images of Superman for the Daily Planet. After our Diana+ design was nailed down and in production, designing an authentic recreation of this incredible flash camera was next on the list.

The original Diana flash gave us the design and shape inspiration for our new DianaF+ flash. We employed a modern capacitor and a single "AA" battery power system. Keeping true to its roots, we opted to keep the original flash's two-pronged "plug" adapter. The existing Diana+ was then retrofitted to accept this unique flash plug and sync perfectly with it. For those wishing to either use the DianaF+ flash on another camera with a standard hotshoe, or to use another hotshoe flash on the DianaF+, we crafted a handy plug-to-hotshoe converter. As icing on the cake, we also engineered a small slot in front of the flash element, allowing it to accept plastic color filters.

Of course, the DianaF+ retained the original innovations of the Pinhole & Endless Panorama. Add that to the staggering possibilities of nighttime, daylight, and color flashing – and you have simply the most flexible and exciting plastic camera ever available.

So far!

The Diana+ System

That "so far" is really key. For this is just the start of a very long journey. You can expect to see a full range of Diana+ accessories, interchangeable lenses, limited editions, seriously exciting camera variants, bags, and a whole lot more heading down the pipeline. We aim to create an entire world around the Diana – a full system that allows you to extend your creative potential to virtually limitless extremes. A comprehensive plastic camera collection the likes of which the world has never seen.

From the day that we received our first film back from the lab, we knew there was no turning back. Long live the Diana!

Diana+ Clones

An Old Tradition

As we mentioned in the history of the original Diana, it was extensively copied and introduced under different names and slightly different physical designs. The lion's share of these copies can be found cataloged in our "Detrich Collection" of classic Diana cameras. Although it's not clear who actually produced these clones, it's accepted that these countless variants are a joyfully collectible and charming aspect of the original Diana. As such, it behooves us to follow the tradition with our own series of special edition and commemorative Diana+ clones. We'll take inspiration, colors, designs, and names from all points, people, and things. We'll produce lots of some, little of others, and unknown quantities of the rest. Some will be available through Lomography, and others through external or even unnamed sources. But one thing is for sure: they will be lovingly cataloged on our ever-growing Diana+ microsite at www.lomography.com/diana

Lomography World Congress 2007 Diana+

Limited edition "MEG" Diana+

London You're a Lady

Hot on the heels of the Diana+'s introduction, we presented the very first clone: the Lomography World Congress 2007 Diana+. Painted in gold and emblazoned with commemorative graphics, this beauty was distributed to all of the Congress participants in London. What the hell happened at the Lomo World Congress 2007? See a full recap of this incredible event at **congress.lomography.com**

Fell in Love with a Girl

For our next Diana+ clone, we couldn't have asked for a better companion. In October 2007, we launched a historic partnership with The White Stripes - one of the most creatively thrilling and sonically stunning rock bands of their time. Singer/guitarist Jack White and drummer/vocalist Meg White are easily recognized for their black, white and red color scheme - which is applied to their clothing, instruments and album art. As part of our collaboration, a limited edition "MEG" Diana+ was created and introduced to the dual communities of Lomographers and fans of The White Stripes. Each "MEG" Diana+ included a custom "Nobody Knows How to Talk to Children" Ringflash, a peppermint swirl filter that mounts behind the lens, a special edition of the Diana+ True Tales & Short Stories book, and a beautiful custom-designed package. Read all about it, and check out our exclusive Lomographic images of The White Stripes live at **www.lomography.com/whitestripes**

Diana Vignettes II

Time for a Walk
By Nick Counts (NicoLomo)

It was a crisp Autumn day when Randy decided that it was time for a walk. This was, of course impossible, because Randy was paraplegic. He had been since birth. Randy was fully aware of this fact, but when he woke up on this particular crisp Autumn morning, he knew that today he would walk.

It might have been part of a lingering dream, permeating his waking thoughts with warm fuzzy feelings that interweave with reality as dreams often do. It may have been the singular quality of the shafts of light, leaking into his room through the venetian blinds and making patterns on his bed. It was as if his room were a Holga and he the precious film inside. In any case, whatever it was that was causing this sudden knowledge of Randy's yet-to-be-accomplished walking feat, he knew that something about this morning was different.

Wiping the sleep from his eyes, Randy sat up in bed and tested his legs. Nope, not yet. He pulled his wheelchair closer to the bed and adeptly maneuvered himself into its seat. He rolled out of his room and into the hall. At the top of the stairs, Randy stopped.

"James!" he called.

James, Randy's older brother by 3 years and 4 months, emerged from his room, looking as though he was still asleep. He walked over to Randy and without a word stooped, lifted Randy (wheelchair and all), and carried him down the stairs. Turning on his heel, James wordlessly sleep-walked back to his room and shut the door.

Randy wheeled himself into the kitchen where his mother was sitting reading the funny pages of the paper. Rolling himself to the only place at the table that lacked a chair, Randy began to eat his breakfast. It consisted of one blueberry pancake, a bowl of oatmeal with brown sugar, and two eggs sunny side up. He wanted to say something to his mother, but she was still reading. He finished eating in silence. Then there was a pause. A moment of no motion. Then Randy spoke up.

"Mom, I'd like a camera for Christmas."
"Santa can't afford a camera," his mother said without looking up from the paper.
"But he can have the elves make it for free."
"He still has to buy the parts. Maybe next year." And that was that.

At school, Randy was unhappy. He sat alone at lunch because nobody would sit with him. This was due partially to the fact that all the students' parents had told them not to stare at Randy because he was in a wheelchair. Well it is very hard to hold a conversation with somebody when you can't look at them and even harder to get to know somebody if you can't talk to them, and therefore, Randy had no friends at school.

Now, as he sat alone, he wondered how he was ever going to get himself a camera. His allowance was 25 cents a week and at that rate, he'd be 50 before he could afford even the cheapest camera.

As Randy was sitting, thinking depressing thoughts, the noise from the cafeteria seemed to build until it reached a crescendo, then it suddenly stopped. All was silent. Randy looked up from his lunch. Standing over him was a girl with blue hair and a black dress.

"May I sit down?" she asked.
"Yes," said Randy.

Randy had never talked to a girl before besides his mother and his physical therapist and neither of them had blue hair. Needless to say, Randy was at a loss for words.

"My name is Diana, what's yours?" the girl said.
"I'm Randy."

They sat wordlessly for a few minutes in which Randy took a few more bites from his cold grilled cheese sandwich and Diana watched him as if she had never seen a boy eat a sandwich before. After this, Diana spoke up.

"Do you want to do something after school?"
"OK," Randy answered.

"Meet me at the front doors," and with that Diana got up and left. Forty five seconds later the bell rang and everybody stood at once. Like sand in an hourglass, the students crowded the doors and funneled into the halls. Randy remained seated. It wasn't time for him to stand. Not yet.

When the final bell rang at the end of the day, Randy went as fast as his wheels would carry him to the front doors. He was nervous, but excited. The prospect of having a friend, however strange she might be, made him very happy.

As he approached the front doors, he distinctly recognized Diana's blue hair through the endless throngs of people trying to be the first to leave the school. Randy pushed through the crowd, running over one boy's foot as he yelled out in pain and surprise. After what seemed like an eternity, he reached the front door where Diana was waiting, seemingly oblivious to all the people trying to squeeze past her.

"Ready to go?" she asked.
"I am very ready," Randy replied.
"Then let's go."

They departed through the front doors and soon the noise of the mobbing students faded in the distance. Diana insisted on pushing him and he was left with his thoughts as they traveled in silence. Randy began thinking of his favorite things and how he could now share them with his new friend. He thought about sunsets on the rocks by the water. He thought about making fires and having warm cocoa on a cold winter day. He thought about laying out under the stars while floating listlessly on the currents of the nearby river. As he thought about these things, Randy smiled to himself. He was very happy now. Surfacing from this thoughts, Randy decided to tell Diana about some of the things that he would like to someday share with her. As he looked up, however, he found the they had walked much farther then he had thought. In fact, he had no idea where they were at all.

"Where are we?" he asked.
"In a corn field," Diana said.

Indeed, they were in a corn field; a clearing in a corn field to be exact.

All around them stalks of corn shot up from the ground, creating a wall from the rest of the world. The midday Autumn sun peered over the wall of corn casting a surreal light into the clearing.

"What will we do here?" Randy asked.
"What do you want more than anything?" Diana asked as if she had not heard his question.
"What?"
"If you could have any one thing in the world, what would it be?"
"Well now that I have a friend, I would like a camera." Randy said.
"What if you didn't have a friend?" Diana pressed.
"What do you mean?"
"I mean if you didn't have a camera and you didn't have a friend, which would you rather have?"

Randy thought about this, but could not decide. He liked having a friend, it was one of the most amazing feelings he had ever experienced, however, if he had a camera he could fulfill his dream of one day becoming a real photographer.

"I can't decide," Randy said at last.
"Well what do you look for in a friend?" Diana asked.
"I look for somebody with whom I can share all the secret wonderful things that I love and that nobody else knows about," Randy replied with vigor.
"And why do you want a camera?"
"So I can one day become a real photographer and so I can capture all the best times, the worst times and just all the times in my life!"
"What if you could have both of those together in one?"
"How--?"

"Close your eyes," Diana interrupted.

Randy closed his eyes. He was unsure what Diana was up to, but he didn't want to disappoint her by opening his eyes. He remained waiting with his eyes closed for what seemed like an eternity. It began to rain and Randy became uncomfortable.

"Diana?" he called out. No answer. He opened his eyes in panic. The light had grown dimmer while he had had his eyes closed. He looked around for Diana, but she was nowhere to be found. In the growing darkness, he scanned his surroundings until something blue on the ground caught his eye. Looking harder in the dim light, he saw what looked like a camera lying a few meters away on the ground. Before Randy knew what he was doing, he felt himself rise from his wheelchair and walk toward the camera. Walking was easy, it was as if he could have walked all along. It felt wonderful to stretch his legs for the first time in his life.

When he reached the camera, he stooped and picked it off the ground. Wiping the rain drops off of it, he examined it. It was mostly black with blue on top. Upon closer examination, Randy noticed that it had a word on the front of the lens. He squinted in the dwindling light to read the word. It said "Diana."

Randy covered Diana with his sweatshirt to protect her from the rain. Turning toward the path to exit the clearing, he began walking home. He felt contented to know that there were many adventures in store for him and his best friend, Diana.

The Goddess of the Hunt
by Regina Belmonte (hydrosuicide)

When she was a little girl, Nancy's aunt told her that photographs were reflections of how the person behind the camera truly saw the person in front of it. She was six. She didn't think much of that little nugget of insight at the time, but nevertheless, when her aunt placed the plastic camera into her hands, her quest to forever capture and immortalize the souls of strangers began.

Diana, goddess of the hunt. It was a fitting name for a camera, she thought years later. She had an entire room in her home devoted to small, square photos of all the faces she had caught on celluloid; the spoils of the hunt.

Nancy's grandmother had died earlier that year, the year she was six. She had never really known death until that cold moment by her Nana's bedside when the doctor said that she was gone, and wide-eyed and afraid, she knew that she had to find some way to keep people in her heart forever.

It began with the people she loved. Her photographs of her brother captured the gaiety and brightness of his wild and carefree personality through his silly antics and his megawatt grin. She took pictures of her bunny; he was sweet and cuddly and loving, and his big fluffy face showed it. Her mother was never more beautiful than in the photos taken by her adoring only daughter. "You must really love me," she once said. She was a believer of Auntie's superstitions as well.

Years passed, and from a girl of six, Nancy grew to a girl of twenty-six, still armed with her fragile plastic soultrap. She had moved on from the things she knew to the things she didn't, still equipped with her keen eye for story and her lust to steal the world away and tuck it into her heart of hearts.

She had the painted, mad lush faces of movie stars, with their deep doe eyes, their tragedy, and their dripping red lips. She had the faces of people on the street, dirty, tired, anonymous, and enduring. She had the innocent smiles and laughter of children who knew not what was ahead, and would someday, sorrowfully, find out. She captured musicians telling the stories of their lives through sound and song. She captured romances, hopelessly doomed. She captured hope, faith, love, sin, and ambition. She and her Diana were the finest of huntresses.

She possessed souls and stories in 5" x 5" prints scattered across whitewashed walls. She had a piece of the heart of the world.

Someone once asked her how she took such evocative photographs. "I see the beauty in everything," she said. "Even in the things that are not beautiful. Because there are no things that are not beautiful."

"Everyone has a story like none other, just as everyone has a face that, once it passes, will never be seen to walk this earth again. You are the only one with a soul like yours. Now, smile!" she said. "Or don't, whichever you prefer." A brief vision of blue and black plastic, and another one for her vast collection.

In her room of photos and faces, she had the world at her fingertips. The stories of the world, stolen forever in the blink of an eye. She possessed souls and stories in 5" x 5" prints scattered across white-washed walls. She had a piece of the heart of the world. But that piece didn't fit into the dark, empty space in her heart that desperately needed to be filled.

"What's missing?" she would ask friends over steaming cups of chocolate and coffee. She had her thousands of photographs, her passion. She had all these lives and the insight and experience they gave her; these lives and their endless wisdom. They never had any answers.

Nancy always ended up eventually forgetting that something was missing. She would get caught up in the hunt, looking for more faces to take, more people to know, more souls to immortalize forever. More truth to tell.

On a drunken, chaotic night at a local rock club, she found herself seated next to a musician she was acquainted (albeit not very well) with. They were both nursing bottles of cold beer, and there were empty shot glasses scattered across the table. She was never very good at staying sane under the influence, but she seemed to be holding her own quite well.

"You know, I know nothing about you," he said, taking a swig of beer. She put her bottle down. "What is there to know? I take pictures," she replied, lifting her camera. It was dark in the club; with the camera in one hand and a bright flash in another, she stole his face.

"You don't just take pictures," he said. "You take the people you photograph. Look, now I'm yours forever." She smiled. He leaned in, as if to kiss her. His face was an inch away from hers, and she breathed the smells of smoke, alcohol, and longing. "I've seen every photo you've ever taken," he whispered. "I own every single book of your work that has been published, every magazine, every print."

"I've seen the lives you have imprisoned in square sheets of paper, and they are beautiful, just beautiful. But what I have never seen," he said, "what I have never seen is your life." And then he kissed her, his lips pressed gently against her own, the cold taste of drink passing from his skin to hers, from hers to his, and when it was over, he told her she was beautiful. "But I don't think you have ever seen it," he said. "You of all people should."

At the end of the night, they exchanged numbers with the promise of drinks and conversation. The promise was enough.

And when Nancy entered her room of photographs, of souls and stories, she picked her Diana up, and for the first time in all her 26 years, pointed it at her own face, clicked the shutter, and finally, finally captured her own soul.

Diana Interviews

Ask the Experts

It takes a special kind of vision to appreciate the Diana. Your average person on the street is not too likely to get all worked up about a completely plastic and fairly goofy looking camera. But keep searching and you'll find a small minority who are absolutely in love with it. They not only recognize and appreciate its massive image-taking potential, but they see nothing but sheer beauty in its retro style and light-as-a-feather body. And every now and then, one of these Diana admirers takes their beloved camera by the shutter switch and does something really amazing with it. We call them the "Diana Experts." Here are three all-plastic-all-stars from their ranks.

Mark Sink

May we introduce you to a true Diana virtuoso, a man who truly "lived the dream" in the 1980s NYC downtown art scene. An unbridled lover of the Diana's quirks, Mark treasured its simple controls, toy-like feel, and lo-fi results. He used its el cheapo plastic lens to capture celebrities like Andy Warhol, Jean-Michel Basquiat, and Grace Jones, and also photographed landscapes, nudes, and a ton of other breathtaking subjects. In the esteemed community of unbelievable Diana artists, he's right up there in the front.

Left to right: **Mark**, Andy, Chris, and Peter

http://gallerysink.com/marksink/index.html

1. When did you first encounter the Diana, and what were your initial impressions of it?

The very first encounter was in the 1960s when my parents got me one. I don't remember using it. It was 20 years later when I found the Diana and its unfinished roll of film inside. I processed them while taking an Art Photography course with Ruth Thorne Thompson. They were images of my mother from knee-height. They blew my mind.That was the start of my reverse technology career. The effect was something that I had never seen. I thought that I was the only one using it for serious art. I later found out that I was far from alone. Books and catalogs had published many dozens of users before me. So, I was the second wave. Holga & Lomo is the third.

2. You used your Diana extensively to document the 1980s New York City art scene. Is there any Diana shot or series with a particularly crazy story around it?

Sneaking into [American abstract artist] Cy Tyombly's private opening at the Museum of Modern Art; you just show the guard at the door your plastic wine cup and they let you right in [laughs]. I shot CY and Steve Martin, Francesco Clemente...lots of big stars that night. They love the Diana, and you can see it in the eyes of your subjects. Plus it gets you close to stars because they see that you are not a journalist with a big-gun camera. It's a "What's that thing?" camera.

I have a lot of stories. One of my favorites is a big job that I got with The New Yorker. It was for a special corporate report illustrating stories of the famous authors they first published before their books came out. People like J.D. Salinger (Catcher in the Rye), Rachel Carson (Silent Spring), Jacobo Timerman (Prisoner Without a Name, Cell Without a Number). It was a big deal, 5-grand-a-day shoot. I showed up at the studio with my Diana around my neck and a hand-held flash. Nothing else! The clients and account executives and creative people waiting for me in the studio were not happy. They could not believe I didn't have any equipment with me. So everyone went home...leaving me with the model. I made some images, developed them and brought them over to the agency. They were busy rummaging through photographer portfolios, looking for my replacement. They all looked over their shoulders in horror at the sight of me coming back. I showed them my contact sheets. With great surprise, they loved them, and [they] all clapped and cheered. And they gave me the rest of the project.

3. Is it more about the photographer or more about the camera?

Oh, it's all about the camera [laughs]. I would have never said that before. Or it's both. Of course concept and craft and personal unique vision is paramount, and with all that -the camera theoretically doesn't really matter. But any of the big, big-time museums and private collections are now all collecting large format 8x10" camera work. My Polaroids from the 1980s are vintage and very valuable now. Even more so – as there is no longer any Polaroid SX-70 film.

4. We have to ask: What did Andy Warhol think of your Diana?

He hated it. He was all about the new and sharp. He didn't like the old romantic feel. "It's so old-fashioned," he would say. He hated soft images. Now, if I showed him romantic hot boys rather than naked girls, then he would have liked it more, I think. He always asked, "Why don't you shoot boys?" He did keep my self-portrait nudes [laughs]! He kept a Diana camera of mine that I gave to him to take pictures with. Later on, after his death, the Warhol foundation called me for my release and permission – and asked if I know what was on the Diana film. I gave Andy the Diana to take some images, and I planned to develop them for him. He never used it, and just placed it in a time capsule around 1983.

5. Could you please craft your own Diana haiku for us (5-7-5 pattern).

flight with light plastic
my love huntress Diana
lightbox of my soul

6. New York City has changed enormously in the past years. What are a few things that you really miss?

Well, I don't go back every other month like I used to. Oh gosh... I miss the '80s. I watched the East Village art scene come and go. Times Square and 42nd Street are all cleaned up now and Vegas-like. Soho lofts used to be cheap. I had a rent-controlled room for 20 years in Chelsea on 21st street and 7th Avenue. $150 a month. It was the bomb! It sat over a quiet backyard garden with nothing but birds singing and leaves rustling. I miss that room. A zillion stories from that place we called the "Room." James Iha of the Smashing Pumpkins loved that room. I just miss being young in NYC, hungry and horny. Most of all, I miss that blind ambition and "I can do anything" feeling. It is probably the same rush for a 20-year old arriving now.

The same rush. The storefronts change. The social cliques change. Editors change. But it's still the same in many ways to the young new generations...now the old, beat-up hippie '80 s survivors like me will say, "Gosh, they just don't have clubs like CBGB's anymore, or Area, or the Mudd Club." Bohemia seems to have all moved across the river a decade or more ago. We, who were hot and wild in the 1980s, are all grumpy old men now. But it's fun to be a living relic from that period [laughs]. People want to interview you!

7. Is the Diana more "I'm So Free" or "Walk on the Wild Side?"

"I am so freeeeee," of course. She is light and fun. People smile when you point her at them. Easy to take anywhere . The plastic sound of the winder is the best.

8. Give us your worst Diana horror story.

Speaking of the funny noisy winder, I was in a high-level press circle once, shooting the Pope's visit to Denver for the New York Times. He was approaching us, and I started winding the Diana camera. Everyone around me stopped and turned around to look at me-and then at my security ID tags-and then at my camera.

And once on another high-profile shoot, I was in front of the president of a giant bank. I showed the Diana to him, giggling while I told him that "This is just a toy camera." Again, that was a big mistake. The client did not get the joke. So now, I always set up the Hasselblad and studio strobes even if I am using the Diana.

Ya, the lens tends to fall out sometimes. The little tabs break. It's happened in front of all sorts of celebs. It gets a big laugh. It even happened in front of the Pope once.

9. Tell us the truly unique characteristics that set the Diana apart from all other cameras.

It does everything cameras are not supposed to do. Vignettes and edge blur. [It has] unreliable shutter speeds. It's fragile. It melts in the sun. It's a reverse. It has a voice of its own. Nancy Burson (www. nancyburson.com) traded me a print of hers for the Arrow (a Diana clone) because she liked its qualities. The Arrow is really poorly made, but the blurring at the edges is more intense.

10. Any words of advice for future Diana shooters?

Concept first! Diana likes low light better than harsh bright days. Diana is a great travel camera and a great wedding camera. It romanticizes the event or touristic wonder of the world. Don't do photojournalism. I don't like anything that has lots of busy blah blah in the pictures. Diana does so well with simple graphic shapes and rhythm. How about the idea of the space between the objects in itself being the subject of an image? And let yourself fail. Diana works because Diana lets you have happy accidents. Accidents are the key to success. One has to learn to let go and fail. We live too much in a failsafe world.

Allan Detrich

Mr. Detrich is a mild-mannered freelance pro photographer by day, and an unbelievably prolific collector of Diana (and Diana clones) at night. Over the past decade, he amassed what is surely the world's most comprehensive and stunning assortment of Diana cameras. This all-plastic treasure trove was coined "The Detrich Collection" and purchased by the Lomographic Society in the Summer of 2007.

http://www.allandetrich.com/

1. You amassed what is surely one of the world's most comprehensive Diana collections. What inspired you to start this staggering task? And when did you begin collecting them?

I started the collection when I attended the Ohio Institute of Photography. We had to use one of the Diana or clone type cameras for an assignment. I loved the dream-like effect and the simplicity of its use. I found different models at flea markets and garage sales. I had maybe 15 different types by the year 2000. But with the invention of the Internet and eBay, my collection grew by leaps and bounds from 2000 to the present. I would look daily on eBay for different names, listed under Diana, and when I found a new name, I would record it and then try to win it for the best possible price.

2. Out of your entire collection of Diana and Diana clones, which camera is your absolute favorite?

I really must say that the Playtime Candid Camera is my favorite Diana clone of all time. It is the one with the red plastic top, in place of the usual boilerplate blue color. I got my hands on one, in a really nice box at a camera show in the year 2002. I paid $97.00 for it and I thought I paid a fortune for it. The red color was so unusual; I thought it was well worth it. I posted the photos on my website, and a month or two later I was offered $500.00 for it by someone in Japan. I knew at that point that I had made a good purchase.

3. Tell us the most insane or hilarious story behind one of your Diana purchases.

I purchased a collection of Dianas and clones from someone who had seen my Diana web page. It consisted of at least 30 cameras - some of which I already had and some of which I did not. But one of the cameras in the collection was the *"Future Scientist Flash"* photography kit. This, as far as I know, is a one-of-a-kind camera and kit. The entire kit had a developing tray, chemical, tongs, instructions, a safelight and more, completely intact. The box was not broken or crushed, and it was an amazing find.

4. Name three solid reasons why every photographer should give the Diana a try.

(1) It is photography at its simplest: No gadgets, no settings or focusing. It lets the photographer concentrate on the subject and composition. (2) The camera is very forgiving; it lets you get away with bad lighting. (3) It levels the playing field for all photographers. It lets the photographer's talent show through because if a photographer can take a great photo with a Diana, he truly is a great photographer.

5. Please give us one juicy tidbit of Diana knowledge that almost no one knows.

Here is a very little know fact about the Sinomax Diana Camera clone in the form of a letter from Maud Ramadan, who is pictured on the side of the box.

From: Maud Ramadan, London England

Hi Allan,

Thanks for your e-mail. Yes, that's me! How astonishing! When I thought about what I would write for you I realized that what I know is a lot about the company and very little about the camera itself. But I'll tell you and hope that some of it is of interest or use to you.

My company was called Sino Trading Company. The company's business was import/export with the Far East - importing from Hong Kong various stuff like plastic flowers, 'fancy goods' and clothing and exporting scientific & agricultural equipment to China (how funny that seems now!).

It was a very small company with two directors, who were cousins, a shipping manager, a transport manager and an accountant, as well as various clerks. I joined it in 1960 straight from school at the age of 16 as a junior clerk and I stayed for 7 years, by which time I had climbed quite well up the ladder. There were about 12 of us to begin with but business boomed and the numbers grew. It was a very happy office. In the mid 1960s several of the girls used to spend their lunch hour at the Cavern, a jazz club a few hundred yards from our office block, listening to various groups, including the Beatles, doing lunch time sessions. I never went - I was a snobby jazz fan and could only deplore their poor taste!

Eventually, the company expanded and moved from Liverpool to an industrial development in Runcorn, further along the Mersey. I left shortly after that.

The managing director was Denis Rattle, a flamboyant character (who reputedly had played jazz piano with the Stanley Black Orchestra), and he dealt with the import business. I worked on this side of the company. His cousin, Ronald Trendell was a gentleman and he ran the export (the serious) side of things – his favorite word was 'efficiency'. The firm was very well run, hence its quiet success. The import side was divided into two sections and (unfortunately for this story) the camera was not handled by my section.

Denis Rattle made periodic trips to Hong Kong where we had 4 main suppliers. I don't know which of these supplied the camera. One day he took me up to the roof of the building where we had our office (the Corn Exchange in Liverpool city centre) and took some photographs of me with his very expensive Leica camera. He didn't tell me why but I was probably about 17 or 18 (judging from the 'blancmange' hair style!) and he was the managing director so I didn't ask. Then some months later the Sinomax camera arrived and there I was on the side of the box. On the other side Denis had placed a picture of his son, Simon, as a baby.

Simon was at that time about 8 or 9, I suppose. He often came into the office with his dad on a Saturday morning, to have a play with the type-writers and to chat to whoever was in that week. We used to play 'com-posers 'which was Simon's made-up game of going through the alphabet and alternately having to find a composer with a name beginning with a particular letter. I don't remember him ever being stuck, whereas I often had to make up a name so he wouldn't win. I never got away with it though – he'd always say, 'That's funny. I've never heard of him.' He inherited his dad's musical talent and became a superb conductor. I remember being overwhelmed at a performance of Porgy & Bess which he conducted at the Liverpool Philharmonic Hall. He is now Sir Simon Rattle, conductor of the Berlin Philharmonic Orchestra.

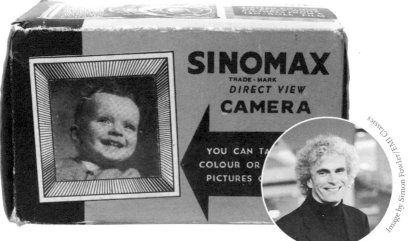

After leaving Sino T.C. I became half of a publishing partnership with a family friend called Fritz Spiegl. He had the ideas for the books about local history and local humor and I did the administration using the good training I had had at Sino TC. So, my career was not as illustrious as my co-star on the Sinomax box, but Scouse Press was good fun for the next few years, until I found my true vocation - as a mother.

That's the background and I'm sorry that I can't tell you any more about the camera itself. As I said, my department didn't handle it so I don't know how many we imported or how many years we sold it. I can't remember it being a runaway success, though. I used to see it occasionally in shop windows in Liverpool and I suppose it was sold throughout the country

I hope there's something of interest that you can extract from these ramblings. You have my picture as a teenager and you asked for a current one for comparison. Unfortunately I can't do this because my computer is primitive and I have no scanner. But if you really think you could use one, my sons have up-to-the minute technology and I could ask one of them to e-mail one to you.

Kind regards,
Maud Ramadan
Thursday, November 25th 2004

6. If the Diana was an animal (land, air, or sea), then what do you feel it would be?

This is a tough question. I think after some deliberation, I would liken it to an alligator. Alligators have poor vision and see images in a blurred fashion. The species overall have not changed much in the scheme of evolution. Like the Diana, it is a basic machine. The camera is used for "snap" shots, likened to the sound of the jaws of the gator on motion, and even one clone is called the "*Snappy.*"

7. What particular personality trait is crucial for taking great Diana shots?

A quick eye and shutter finger; imagination; and an artful eye.

8. Do you feel that the Diana lends itself more to color or black and white shots? Why?

I think that Diana photographs look better in B&W. Black and white is more forgiving and this is needed when photographing with the Diana camera. More can be done with contrast and this makes a good Diana camera image really pop.

9. If the director of the Great Wall Plastics Factory was sitting right next to you, then what would you want to tell him?

I would like to get the figures on how many of the Diana cameras vs. the different clones have been produced in the past. It always amazes me that a Diana camera will sell for nearly $100.00 on eBay, when a rarely seen clone will sell for just $25.00 or less. I can almost guarantee you that there are fifty times more Diana cameras on the market than clones, but people want the "Diana" name.

10. Any words of advice for new Diana shooters?

Use any of the Diana, or Diana clones; they are all the same camera and give the shooter basically the same effect. If you are looking for different effects, try different cameras. All vary slightly, but just going for the Diana camera for the "Diana" name can cost you a bundle. You can usually buy a couple of clones for the price you will pay for a "Diana," this will let you experiment more while finding your own style in the toy camera area.

Tony Lim

Tony Lim is a true master of the analog universe. As both a big-time collector and a no-holds-barred shooter of the Diana camera, he knows this little plastic hermano inside and out. He's amassed over 100 Diana cameras and Diana clones in his personal collection, and organized a personal exhibition of Diana cameras and photos entitled "Hong Kong Toy Camera Photography." You might also know him as a key motivator of the Worldwide Pinhole Day. As a visual and product designer - and a university instructor, he's uniquely qualified to clue us in on the Diana's original concept and positioning. Soak up some expert words from Master Lim below.

http://diana.com.hk
http://holga.com.hk

1. We are very curious to know as many details as possible about the Diana camera. First off, could you tell us how long the cameras were produced, and where they were sold?

According to a Hong Kong government catalog, the Diana was first introduced by the Great Wall Plastics Co. in the early 1960s. The factory was located in Hong Kong's Kowloon City. This time was a sort of "golden age" for the country's plastic industry. Great Wall was one of those common, family-run factories - and was not a precise or high-tech optical plant.

In addition to the Great Wall factory, there was at least one other company in Macau that produced Diana's and Diana clones. There may have been more - but who's to know?

The main market was definitely the United States. Hence, the cameras were produced with English writing and the distance scale was printed in feet, not meters. It's tough to gauge the exact year that Diana production stopped, but it's most likely the mid-to-late 1970s.

2. What was the idea and concept behind the Diana? Was it heavily inspired by the Fujipet, or by another simple 120 cameras of its time?

No I don't believe that the Diana had particular relationship to the Fujipet. Overall, these simple 120 film cameras were very common in the '60s. However, I do feel that the Diana was heavily influenced by the Agfa Isoly. Both cameras were 4x4cm format. And all the handles, levers, and controls are in a very similar position. The main difference is that the Isoly had two shutter speeds: 1/30 and 1/100s.

The idea and concept for the Diana was simply to be a toy or a give-away. It certainly wasn't precise. It seems that most Dianas had little to no quality control for their optics. That's what makes them so unpredictable!

3. How about marketing and advertising? How was the camera generally presented to its customers? Any crazy stories, collaborations, or sponsorships connected to the Diana's promotion?

As far as I know, the retail price for the Diana was about $0.99 USD in the 60s. It was presented as a toy or a simple giveaway. The packaging was very simple, usually a cardboard box or plastic blister pack. It's probably that most Diana owners never even put a roll of film inside their camera.

The Diana was popular as an OEM [original equipment manufacturer] product. This means that outside firms would contract with the Great Wall factory to produce cameras with their brand names. Hence, there are Diana's that say Reader's Digest, Shell, etc.

4. What was the scope of the Diana's production? Can you estimate about how many cameras were produced? How about the size and number of employees of the Great Wall Company?

Great Wall was probably a small factory. Only a few workers would have been required to produce a ton of Diana's. Most of the HK plastic factories at the time were small and family owned.

The total amount of Dianas produced is impossible to count. I can't even imagine how many were made! For a cheap camera made 40 years ago, you can still easily find deadstock pieces which have never been opened or used. The production volume must have been huge! We know that a lot of Converse Chuck Taylor's were made, too, but you can't find deadstock Chuck's as easy as [you can find] Dianas.

5. There are so many Diana variants and copies out there, and we know that you've owned quite a few of them. Can you estimate about how many variants there are? Any idea how many separate factories actually produced these copies - and what their names were? And which variant is your all-time favorite?

At the very least, there were more than 100 variants. I personally have about 80 to 100 Diana clones with at least some difference between them. At least the packaging design and graphics are different.

In terms of actual tooling and camera functions, there were probably very few basic variants on the original Diana. My personal favorite is the all-original Diana. But I also really want one of the Dianas which were made in Macau. They are super rare.

6. When the camera was first released, what did everyone think of its pictures? Did they appreciate the Diana's photo quality and effects?

I doubt that most Dianas were ever used as serious cameras. I've tried out so many of them, and nearly every one has a focus problem, light leaks, or other quality issue. It's almost impossible to find two of them with the same photo outcome. Every Diana was unique, and a bit unreliable in its own special way.

If it was considered a real camera, then they probably wouldn't have made so many of them so cheaply. I believe that most of them were given to children to play with, and [that the] film was never actually placed inside.

In the 1970s, late into the Diana's production run, there was a magazine talking about "Diana Photography." In the story, a professor used a Diana to teach the basic principles of photography to his students. With the Diana, he suggested that they could forget about function and merely concentrate on the act of shooting. You can just focus on the image and the concept behind it. So in that way, the Diana's sheer simplicity was appreciated.

7. The Diana ultimately became an extremely desirable cult item for artistic-minded photographers. But who was their original target customer?

With a retail price of $0.99USD and a wholesale around $0.25, it was definitely positioned as a toy. And given the sheer volume of dead-stock still available, it probably wasn't too successful overall. There's a lot of stock that wasn't sold to end customers!

However, as the plastic cost was so low, and the OEM market so robust, it's possible that the item was profitable. The factory certainly never treated it like a real camera or gave it any serious quality control. A quality German-made folding Agfa camera retailed for $2.99 USD at the time, only three times as much as the toy-like Diana. If people wanted a real camera, they probably spent the extra money on something like that.

8. You've shot a ton of amazing images with the Diana camera. What do you consider its most appealing attributes?

There are two very important things. First, the camera has a lot of unexpected defects. This gives you a lot of possibilities for an interesting result. Diana images match the outcome of "Pictorialism," where the fine art feelings of the photograph - soft focus, dreamy colors, etc. - look a bit like a painting and are more important than the subject itself. Diana shots have that same strong impact.

Second, the Diana offers a "clearance" of your soul and mind. It's simple to use, and enables you to detach yourself from the photograph process. Even if the shot's not in focus, your brain is!

9. Vintage Diana cameras currently sell for around $100 on the used market. What do you think the original designers and producers at the Great Wall Plastic Factory would think of that?

They would never believe it! It's true that design items will have a life of their own. The creators can't forecast the future 40 years ahead.

10. In today's world of digital photography, do you feel that the Diana is still relevant? Why?

Both digital and analog photography have a great market and

relevance, and are very connected. When digital photography grows strong, then the need for new analog photography techniques grow strong as well. Once they experience it, many people fall in love with this new sense of photography. With the supply of photographic equipment and possibilities going up [given digital technology], the demand for all kinds of new experiences [like the Diana] will go up as well.

Cat Ong

Cat Ong lives and works in Hong Kong. His life story reads like this: "I was born in the same month as the Canon AF35M, in Kowloon/ Hong Kong near the production town of the Holga and the Diana. I bought my first camera at the age of 10; after that the situation totally lost control and I started to collect, eat and sleep with cameras. In 2000 I met LC-A while I was studying in Beijing. In 2001 I began dating the Horizon 202 during an exchange programme in Coventry in the UK. Later I worked as a journalist and, again, was involved in writing little stories about camera history. In 2006 I got my dream job as a product developer at the Lomographic Society International. What do I do there? Of course, again, cameras, cameras, cameras..."

1. Please briefly give us the background story of how the Diana+ was created.

I first came to know this project in May 2006. We took a year to research, analyze, and develop the new concept of the Diana+. At the very beginning, we tested a lot of original Diana's. To make sure that we could get what you and me want.

Around this time, we were enjoying success with the newly reborn Lomo LC-A+. We like the concept of "+." We started to think that this new idea could be applicable with a "Diana+"

Meanwhile, we received the very first Diana+ factory sample with the maximum exposure area of 46.5 x 50mm. Our first task was to enlarge the exposure area to nearly the standard 6 x 6cm format. Then we designed the removable lens system and the pinhole function. Finally, we added in the long-exposure shutter lock and the tripod mount for shooting pinhole images. I can also tell you this: at this very moment there is a design for a future accessory within the camera already. You'll come to know this new accessory very soon!

2. What's up with the Diana+'s unique "star shaped" rear shutter?

Ah yes, the camera's shutter has a round circle with four corners. It looks like the combination of a circle and a square. There is an interesting story there!

The original Diana camera of the 60s was designed for the 4 x 4 (42 x 42mm) format. When we re-designed it as the Diana+, we found that there is a lot of space inside the camera body that we could use to make the exposure area larger, without actually increasing the camera's size.

The very first factory sample had only two formats: 46.5 x 50 format without frame (we eventually made this into the 46.5 x 46.5mm panorama format) and the 42 x 42mm original Diana format. Later I measured it in detail again and tried to make the internal exposure area as large as possible. I crafted a handmade sample that can shoot 6 x 7 format within the same Diana+ body. Finally, we decided to make a maximum 6 x 6 format (52mm x 52mm). This second lot of samples have a typical circular rear shutter. But as this shutter was cutting off some light at the corners, you would see "hard black vignetting" at the edges of your image. If you look at the original Diana+ book, you'll see that most of the pictures have this effect – as we were shooting with the second round of sample cams! We modified the shutter and added the extra corners to the circle in order to let in more light and yield a natural vignette look.

3. What was the most difficult characteristic of the original Diana to replicate?

First would be image quality. This is similar to the problem we faced when we had to replicate the exposure control of the LC-A+. There are no standards of image quality for the original Diana camera. Every Diana was different. It's very hard for the factory to replicate the images without a prior standard. So we bought a lot of Diana's on Ebay and tested them out. Finally, we had an idea for the characteristic look and feel of the typical Diana lens. It's relatively sharp in the center, has blurry vignetting at four corners, has very strong colors.

Second (the second most difficult) was to replicate the form of the camera and its original functions. The details were really hard here. Like the feeling of switching the B/N shutter and the Aperture setting. It can't be too loose or too hard. Also, we had to recreate the sound of the shutter. Even the sound of winding on the film. We believed that the hardcore Diana shooters would not be happy if we didn't try our best with these small details.

4. What makes the Diana+ unique from other plastic cameras?

The most important thing is the last century smell of the 60s. The style is a very original example of the 60s "Plastic Era." The Diana+ does not really feel like a camera. It is also not simply a "toy camera" (at least, not for me.) It is truly a tool – a friend to visualize your mind. At first, you will find it difficult to handle. That's because we must apply reason and common skill to use this camera. Everyone will have a basic understanding of the Diana+. If you've never used a film camera before, then this will really contrast with everything else you've shot. After a few rolls of film, or after dating a few Diana+ cameras, you'll find that this tool will fix your life.

5. In addition to wrangling the technical details of the Diana+, you've been one of its most prolific test photographers. What are your favorite techniques?

Haha, shoot under the sun!
I also enjoy to shoot it with the Ringflash and a "B" shutter to get some nice party and night shots.

6. Name three people (living or deceased) who you would like to photograph. Who are they and why?

In keeping with the "Diana+" I choose three girls:

1st is my girlfriend Ceci. She is a home décor editor for a magazine in Hong Kong. She is the most important model for me (in fact you can see her a lot in the first Diana+ book)

2nd is Teresa Tang, a very famous Taiwanese singer of the 70'. She was the first Asian singer who could hit all the markets in Mainland China, Hong Kong, Taiwan and even in Japan. This year is the 10th anniversary of her death. There was even a Japanese TV series about her. I still listen to her vinyls every night.

3rd is Norah Jones. Everyone knows her around the world. I like her very much – both her angel's voice and her look. I saw her photos in Wong Kar Wai's movies "My Blueberry Nights". I wish I could shoot her with the Diana+. I think it will be nice to shoot her big eyes with the Diana+ and Ringflash.

7. How about the DianaF+ Flash? What was it like to re-create the retro look and classic "pin" plugs of that item?

It was a lot of fun to create the DianaF+ and Flash. First we asked the question: How do we want to flash to flash on the Diana+?

The quickest and easy way would be: add a standard "hotshoe" to the Diana+. Everyone knows how to use it. It is also the cheapest way for manufacturing as the parts are very easy to find.

However, we finally decided to 99% recreate the original "pin" plug system and retro look of the 60s Diana flash. That is important for the Diana+ rebirth project. To keep things as original as possible. To remake the classic idea in a new context.

We are very lucky that the original shape of the Diana flash is quite large. We had enough space to redesign the model structure inside of it. Our modern pin plug is made of very good materials, so its like the old one but more safe.

8. You've been a pro photographer for quite a few years. What's the strangest assignment that you've been given?

Reporting spa facilities in Sri-Lanka...
Or reporting the Euro 2004 in Portugal – starting as a idiot of soccer and finally becoming a true football fan...
Or reporting the birth of Nil (son of Lomography's Sally Bibawy and Matthias Fiegl) in Vienna in 2005...

9. If you could create the perfect Diana+, what features would it have?

I'm not sure that I can mention these ideas here, can I?

I can surely tell you that there will be a lot more sweet accessories coming out soon. Diana+ is not simply a plastic toy camera. It is a full compact 120 format camera system that represents analog photography style NOW. As you can see, the foundations of an interchangeable lens system are already there. You can bet that there will be some nice lenses for it. For me, the Diana+ is a lovely light box with film transport that can make any possibility.

10. Any last words of advice for the Diana+ shooters out there?

If you are a pro Diana+ shooter, I don't have much to offer. Enjoy and you know you can't get rid of it.

If you are a new Diana+ shooter or just got your Diana+ and haven't yet shot a roll, then save the first roll for a sunny day. You will fall in love with this lovely girl immediately. It doesn't means you can't shoot in the dark or on rainy days. Just make sure that you can get that successful feeling the first time.

The Detrich Collection

Feast your eyes!

Thank god for the Internet. By tirelessly searching its many hidden nooks and crannies – and by placing a hell of a lot of Ebay bids – Mr. Allan Detrich was able to amass what must be the most incredible, diverse, and mouth-watering collection of Diana cameras and Diana clones in the entire world. In Spring 2007, the Lomographic Society purchased this incredible batch of plastic and is absolutely thrilled to present it as the priceless "Detrich Collection." A taste of the Hong Kong treats that await your inspection, can be found at www.lomography.com/diana. And keep your schedule open, as we intend to display this collection through a worldwide traveling exhibition. It might be coming to a major city, rustic small town, or backwater swamp near you!

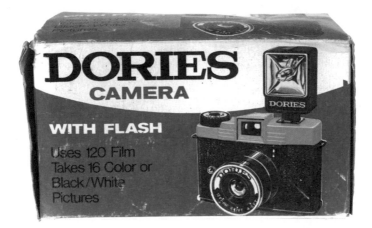

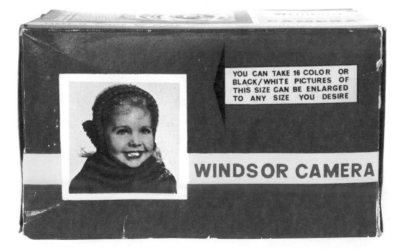

Diana Vignettes III

Manny Royo vs. the Undead
By Michael Kuhle (username: michaelkuhle)

Manny really missed Luquillo beach. For the past ten years – ever since he was a teenager – he worked in this idyllic spot in Northeast Puerto Rico. White, soft sand and calm, azure water for as far as the eyes could see. That place was really easy on the eyes. So were the girls for that matter. He was quite the playboy in his time, and none of his amigos thought a woman could tie him down. That was, until lovely & blond Linda came into his life.

Ahh, Linda. He remembers the first time that American gringa crossed his path. Long, slender legs. Wavy hair that would put a Pantene model to shame. Say what you want about love at first sight, but this was the real thing. She nearly knocked him out of his lifeguard chair, and it was only moments before he was sauntering down the beach to find out her name. One thing led to another, one week led to one month, and one chance meeting led to Manny moving in with his gorgeous and quite serious girlfriend – back in her hometown of New York City. He didn't have much to his name, so he packed light. Just a few shirts, a couple of pants, a decent selection of socks, underwear, and unmentionables, and his uncle's clunky plastic camera. Sure, this thing wasn't a Hasselblad – but Manny couldn't really afford better for the moment, and he wasn't a photographer anyhow. This dusty old "Diana" camera served him just fine for the occasional snapshot – even if developing its crazy film was kind of a pain in the ass.

The big move was a few months ago, in the blazing heat of the Puerto Rican summer. Today, Manny is strutting up Lexington Avenue on a cool New York Fall day, heading over to meet his girlfriend. She mans one of the cosmetics counters at Bloomingdales, and has been known to really blow out her share of Bobbi Brown lip gloss and moisturizer. For Manny's part, he's holding down a part-time temp job and seriously enjoying his life with Linda, his dream girl. He loves to surprise her in the middle of her shift with a sloppy kiss and a cheap rose from the corner convenience store. As he selects the best looking flower from a white bucket, he hears a crazy noise from man a little bit down the street.

Uuuuugggggghhhhhhhh...

"Ay carbon, this guy is drunk," thinks Manny. He can't even see his face, but it's obvious that the dude in front of him is really hammered. He's all hunched over and breathing crazy. From the back of him, it looks like there's a decent amount of tomato sauce ...or maybe that's blood!... on his shirt. Manny examined him with equal parts sympathy and disgust until he turned around.

Whoa! Dios mio! What the hell's going on here!!?! The face that married the moan was clearly missing a few pieces. Like a right eye, and half a left cheek. And a nose. This guy was more than sick, he was literally decomposed. On top of that, it looked like he brought a few friends along. Right behind him was about a dozen ...no a hundred! ... similarly decrepit and feral animated bodies. Even if New York can get a little crazy at times, this clearly wasn't business as usual.

Manny was a child of the Eightes. He wasn't a babe in the woods, and he knew exactly what was up. ZOMBIES!! Clearly, some kind of toxic gas or liquid had been released accidentally [or intentionally!] and brought the dead back to life. Dawn of the Dead, 28 Days Later – hell, even Thriller – had prepared him for this moment. He knew Armageddon when he saw it shuffling down the street.

Conventional weapons wouldn't work against them. You can't smack them with a bat or hit them with a car. They're already dead! Manny knew full well what he had to do. SHOOT THEM IN THE BRAIN. That, and get Linda out of here with a quickness.

That was easier said than done. They nearly had Bloomie's surrounded already! He knew that fighting them in close quarters would be problematic, but if he could confront them on the street – then he could outmaneuver them. As he already knew, zombies are pretty slow-moving and slow-witted. *"OYE!! MIRA!!"* screamed Manny! He had to distract them from going in the East door – that's a little too close to where Linda manned the cosmetics counter. The zombies looked at Manny and sensed that this plucky guy most likely had a great-tasting cabeza. "BRAINS!!" they cried, as they turned away from the door and lurched towards him. Men, women – young and old alike – with all manner of festering wounds, amputated limbs, threadbare clothing, and desperate, rotten faces followed Manny and his klaxon call.

But there was a little problem here. Manny wasn't Bruce Willis or 50 Cent. It's not like he packed a handgun for his date – or even owned one. If shooting them in the brains was the only option, then how was he going to fight them? For a fleeting second, a crazy idea came to him. "No, that couldn't work," he thought. But as a blonde-haired corpse with a see-through hole in her stomach reached out for him, he figured that it was worth a try. "The only thing that I can shoot them with is *mi tio's* Diana camera," he concluded. In a flash, he loaded it up, took aim, and fired!!

And wouldn't you know it! The first shot rang true, and the blonde zombie dropped dead [again!]. Next, he took out a rotted construction worker, a brain-crazed chef, a deceased punk-rock ingénue, a blood-splashed nurse, and a guy who looked a hell of a lot like Hunter S. Thompson. As long as he passionately composed the image through his viewfinder – aiming straight at the head – each click of the Diana was a good as a silver bullet to the brain. Lucky for Manny – he brought plenty of ammunition along – in the unassuming form of medium format film rolls.

But even this one man "Rambo" couldn't take on the whole zombie horde. For each undead being that he dropped, another one popped into its place from somewhere in the rear. He needed some help. A few cops were out on the street – firing their automatic handguns in vain. All of their shots hit the typical "center mass" which was as good as tossing plantain chips at these hardened corpses. Manny called at them to shoot for the head, but they weren't listening to them. Instead he popped into what must be the last remaining one-hour photo development stop in this midtown neighborhood. A humble little store owned by Mr. and Mrs. Park.

As you would understand, this elderly Korean couple was a bit skeptical. Oh yeah – they saw the bloodthirsty gang of zombies outside their window. They heard their desperate calls for "BRAINS!" and "THE LIVING!" And no, they sure as hell didn't believe that this admittedly suave Latino man was taking them out with a 40-year old plastic camera. But Manny proved his point by aiming out the window and taking down a few of them on the sidelines. Two ugly guys and a girl – to be exact. Mr. Park couldn't believe his eyes, but there was no denying it. In the entire history of the occult, here was the first rampaging pack of literally photo-sensitive undead that the world had ever known. Luckily, this one-hour photo shop was the rough equivalent of a fully stocked armory. Mr. and Mrs. Park grabbed a fistful of slide films, punched them into multiple auto-advancing cameras, and followed Manny outside – teeth gritted, hearts steeled, and camera–guns blazing.

Oh, it was a massacre. Between the three of them, the zombies didn't stand a chance. The horde dropped like flies as shots of Provia, Velvia, Superia, Ektachrome, CT Precisa, and some cheap crap that expired in 1997 quickly thinned their ranks. Within the space of a few minutes, the entire mass of zombies had been eliminated – right down to the very last blood–sucker. Manny surveyed the scene and basked in his triumph. With the help of old–school film technology, he and the Parks saved New York City and defeated the powers of death. Not only that – he was going to quite literally have the pictures to prove it!

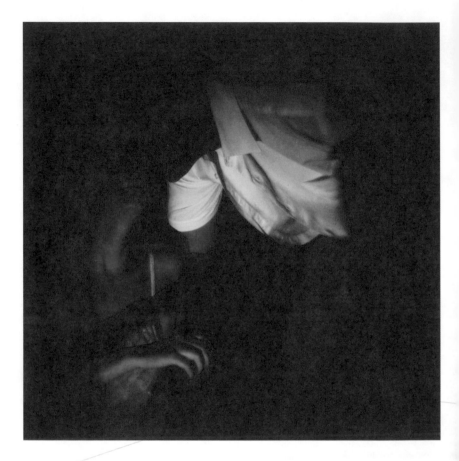

Diana Online

Diana in Digital

It's a bit ironic to think that one of the world's most "analog" creations would have such a massive amount of electronic content dedicated to its past, present, and future. But it makes perfect sense: After all, the Diana is ultimately a dynamic, unpredictable, inspirational, and sometimes frustratingly blurry tool for hyperactive Lomographers around the world. It's only fitting that a robust and dynamic website be dedicated to the task of summing up everything Diana-related and cranking it out in delicious bite-sized morsels for your constant consumption. We like to call this the "Diana Microsite." To find it, just go out your front door, make a left, walk three blocks down, catch the "13A" crosstown bus, take five steps backward with your eyes closed and your left finger on your nose, and you'll arrive right in front of this address: <u>www.lomography.com/diana</u>.

Once you've wiped your feet, taken off your hat, and stepped inside, you'll be delighted to find the following waiting for you:

- The interactive Diana Vignette Challenge, where you can contribute corresponding Diana images to a collection of short stories (and where you can submit stories too if ya like).
- The most comprehensive collection of Diana tips, tricks, techniques, and collective knowledge on Earth.
- Fascinating interviews with world-renown Diana Experts.
- The tantalizing "Detrich Collection," the world's most stunning assortment of vintage Diana cameras and Diana clones.
- Extensive Diana photo galleries which can pretty much knock you head over arse.
- The latest updates on the next Diana World Tour location!
- All manner of networking possibilities with like-minded Diana folks.

And in addition all of this Diana-related material, you might like to pay a visit to a few other noteworthy spots in our Lomographic online world:

Our online Lomographic shop – open 24 hours a days, every day
shop.Lomography.com

Your very own one-room-mansion in our Lomographic world, where you can put your best shots on the walls
www.lomohomes.com

A Constantly Updated and Completely Irresistible List of Lomographic Events
www.lomography.com/events

The Most Unbelievable and Hugely Inspiring FREE Photo Competitions Ever Seen
www.lomography.com/missions

Our Very Friendly and Local-Active Asian Partner Websites

Japan: **www.lomography.jp**
South Korea: **www.lomography.co.kr**
Asia Pacific: **www.lomographyasia.com**

The Lomographic Society

The Lomographic Society // How Everything Started

In the early 1990s, a handful of Viennese students took a trip to Prague and happened upon a small enigmatic Russian camera called the Lomo Kompakt Automat. Immediately, they started a new style of artistic experimental photography using their unorthodox snapshot cavortings. Their approach: Take as many photographs (Lomographs) as possible in the most impossible of situations possible and from the most unusual positions possible and having them developed as cheaply as possible. The result was a flood of authentic, colorful, crazy, off-the-wall, and unfamiliar snapshots, which could be combined and mounted on panels to form a sea of thousands of Lomographs. Lomographic events, exhibitions, and interactive projects were soon rolled out across the world, and Lomographic "Embassies" were founded in over 75 countries. To date, major shows have been held in Moscow, New York, Vienna, Berlin, St. Petersburg, Paris, Shanghai, Guangzhou, Bangkok, Kuala Lumpur, Sidney, Melbourne, Sao Paolo, Rio de Janeiro, Mexico City, Guadalajara, Medelin, Toronto, Oslo, Stockholm, Malmö, Helsinki, Cape Town,

Johannesburg, Seoul, Havana, Zurich, Cologne, Madrid, Cairo, Frankfurt, Dubai, Oslo, Tokyo, Hong Kong, Singapore, Buenos Aires, London, Barcelona, Beijing, and many other cities. In fact, you might want to cast a quick glance at **www.lomography.com/ events** to see what's going down at this very moment.

Lomography people, lifestyle, and tools

What started out as a spontaneous artistic approach to photography in the Vienna underground scene developed into an international socio-cultural movement, one that uses photography as a creative approach for capturing the world - and for communicating with others. Today, we are a globally active organization dedicated to experimental and creative snapshot photography. Boasting more than 500,000 active members across the world, the idea of Lomography encompasses an interactive, democratic, social, cultural, vivid, blurred, and crazy way of life.

This development is supported and furthered by the creation of special tools that were either discovered or specifically designed and manufactured. We're mostly talking affordable snapshot cameras like the Lomo LC-A, the four-lensed Supersampler & Actionsampler, the Colorsplash and Fisheye cameras, and the Holga and Horizon cameras. But there's also a whole assortment of accessories, including flashes, tripods, films,; fantastic in-house published books; and awesome fashion items to discover as well. Check out the whole assortment on **www.lomography.com**.

Lomography & visual culture

The social and visual credo of Lomography has influenced lots of different people - from cultural gurus and creative types to business people, educators, and other professionals. Among these strident supporters and Lomographic camera shooters are quite a few celebrities and well-known creative types, such as Moby, David Byrne, LCD Soundsystem, Vladimir Putin, Master Yuen, Underworld, Giovanni Ribisi, Nobuyoshi Araki. Franz Ferdinand, Dalek, Eve, Anton Corbijn, Daft Punk, Danny Clinch, Nikki Sixx, Staple Design, Rosie O'Donnell, Jeanne Tripplehorn, Yonehara Yasumasa, Mark Romanek, Jason Lee, Shepard Fairey, Kirsten Dunst, the White Stripes, Kozyndan, Eva Mendes, Bady Minck, the Leningrad Cowboys, and Meatloaf. So you're in good company!

The Lomographic credo - "be fast, be open-minded, be communicative" - has spread into an approach that is shared throughout the Lomographic network. This creative premise is based on the playful combination of lo-tech and hi-tech, and the amalgamation of a cultural institution with a commercial photographic and design company. This grants our Lomographic Society an exquisite role in this age of borderless global telecommunications wherever images and visual language are involved.

The 10 Golden Rules of Lomography

As you embark on your road of Lomographic discovery, you'll undoubtedly be the multi-camera-bearing fool at every party, the person who walks around a foreign city all night for the perfect low-light shot, the maniac who sits at a noodle joint by themselves and photographs their own chopsticks, the heavy-hitter whose bag never has less than five cameras and a dozen rolls of film, and the severely lucky ducky who records each and every moment of their life with a stream of some of the most amazing and mind-blowing analog images that have ever been created. While you travel this path, here are a few pearls of wisdom to guide you. They worked pretty well for us.

1. Take your camera everywhere you go.
2. Use it anytime, day and night.
3. Lomography is not an interference in your life, but a part of your life.
4. Try the shot from the hip.
5. Approach the objects of your Lomographic desire as closely as possible.
6. "Don't Think" (William Firebrace).
7. Be fast (we can't stress that enough).
8. You don't have to know beforehand what you've captured on film...
9. ...and you don't necessarily have to know afterwards, either.
10. Don't worry about any rules.

The Lomography World Archive & Lomography.com

Where is all of this going? We are busy-beavering away with hundreds of thousands of Lomographers on the perpetually ongoing Lomographic Sisiphus project: The Lomography World Archive. This archive seeks to document the incredible world around us in a never-ending stream of snapshots, and we hope to make it the biggest and most dazzling snapshot collection on Earth, a collection of millions of the wackiest, most exciting, and most impressive sights and moments of our time! Where are these archives? Inside the shoe boxes of Lomographers, stacked on chairs or tables, in cupboards, drawers, albums, on the ceilings and walls, cataloged on computer hard drives, in the vast collections of the Lomographic Embassies and at the Lomographic Society International Central Office in Vienna... and in the highest & most selective quality at the online LomoWorldArchive at **www.lomography.com/archive**. It's an archive that's growing by the minute!

Join the Lomographers, and discover all the events, competitions, activities, products, and inspirational bits and pieces that we offer. We can't wait to meet you!

Our International Website
www.lomography.com

The Extremely Receptive and Gregarious E-mail Address for all of your Questions
contact@lomography.com

Lomographic Society Offices Worldwide

Hey, if you're ever in the neighborhood, then feel free to pop by one of our warm-hearted Lomographic offices. Bring your personal Lomographic portfolio, some baked goods or an extremely cute puppy and you're guaranteed to catch us in a fantastic mood.

Europe
Lomographic Society International
Hollergasse 41, A-1150 Vienna
tel: +43.1.899 44 0
fax: +43.1.899 44 22
contact@lomography.com

USA
Lomographic Society USA
20 JAY STREET, # 314
Brooklyn, NY 11201
tel: +1.718. 522 4353
fax. 718. 522 4468
info-usa@lomography.com

Japan
Lomographic Society Japan
3-13-23 Minami-Aoyama
3rd Floor
Minato-ku Tokyo 107-0062
tel/fax: +81.3.5772 7867
www.lomography.jp

Korea
Lomographic Society Korea
1F 362-14, Seogyo-dong Mapo-gu,
121-838 Seoul, South Korea
 tel: +82-2-522-0255
fax: +82-2-523-0255
www.lomography.co.kr

Hong Kong
Lomography Asia Pacific Ltd.
No.2, G/F Po Yan Street,
Sheung Wan,
Hong Kong
tel: +852 2525 5417
fax: +852 2525 5467
info@lomographyasia.com

Credits and Resources

Credits

Published by the Lomographic Society International
Copyright Lomographic Society International 2007

Diana F+ camera design and concept by Lomographic Society International
Vignettes by Michael Kuhle, Sarah Zucker, Nick Counts, & Regina Belmonte

Image Credits
The gorgeous images pasted throughout this book (with the exception of the images within "Diana Interviews") are courtesy of the following ultra-talented photographers:

Name	Username	Country
Federico Abrigo	dczypher	Philippines
Corinne Baudevin	azurblue	France
Regina Belmonte	hydrosuicide	Philipines
Peter Boesch	ringo	Paris
Cristin Bowman	laughing_fig	USA
Pan Chan	panism	Hong Kong
Anna Clem	aapertura	USA
Helen Errington	scootiepye	United Kingdom
Daniel Felmer	danika	Austria
Matthias Fiegl	fiegl	Austria
Eriko Fujita	eriejetcity	USA
Julia Jachs	julialomo	Austria
Elisabeth Jarmer	lis_ette	Austria
Stephan Kaps	mephisto19	Germany
Chinarat Kl	panoraman	Thailand
Michael Kuhle	michaelkuhle	USA
Paul Lavallee	mylatehope	USA
Yi-Chuan Lu	alice26992	Taiwan
Katharina Machu	_ka_	Austria
Severin Matusek	severin	Austria
Hind Mezaina	hind	UAE
Monika Mitterdorfer	agrimony	Austria
Denis Montillet	DenisM	France
Tracy V. Moore	tracyvmoore	USA
Daisuke Naminoue	daisuke	Japan
Cat Ong		Hong Kong
Pat Padua	squadoosh	USA

Sofia Plana	almudein	Spain
Steffi Plattner	die_steffi	Italy
Adam Scott	adamscott	United Kingdom
Chomdee Smith	chomdee	United Kingdom
Mandi Steininger	mandi	Austria
Cameron Stephen	artpunk	Australia
Mark Warner	warnerm	USA
David Wilms	007-0815-Styler	Germany

Diana Interview Participants

A huge thanks to Mark Sink, Allan Detrich, Tony Lim & Cat Ong for the images and insights that they contributed to their respective interviews.

Fiction Disclaimer

The Diana Vignette short stories included in this book are purely fictional. Any references to actual persons, living or deceased, are intended for entertainment and parody.

Additional Reading

Spend a little time on the Internet and school yourself on the Diana and Diana+ by visiting these tasty and informative sites:

http://en.wikipedia.org/wiki/Diana_camera
The ever-changing and always-expanding Wikipedia entry for the Diana

http://en.wikipedia.org/wiki/Medium_format_(film)
A mighty nice Wikipedia entry on medium format film (the Diana's favorite!)

http://www.toycamera.com/diana/
General Diana info & a great collection of all the different Diana variants and copies

http://www.huskudu.com/guide.html
Beautiful Diana photographs and a scanned original instruction booklet

http://www.dianacamera.com/
Kai Yamada's gorgeous Diana image portfolios

http://www.collection-appareils.com/diana/html/diana.php
A quite nice collection of Diana camera varieties, mostly in French

http://www.merrillphoto.com/Dianas.htm
Two absolutely priceless videos of dancing Diana cameras. We're not joking

http://www.flickr.com/groups/dianaphotos/
Online discussion group dedicated to the original Diana camera
(Flickr membership required)

http://www.flickr.com/groups/diana_plus/
Online discussion group dedicated to the Diana+ & DianaF+ camera
(Flickr membership required)